Original title:
Tropical Blue and Golden Glow

Copyright © 2025 Creative Arts Management OÜ
All rights reserved.

Author: Mariana Leclair
ISBN HARDBACK: 978-1-80581-647-8
ISBN PAPERBACK: 978-1-80581-174-9
ISBN EBOOK: 978-1-80581-647-8

Azure Embrace at Sunrise

As dawn ticks, the sky does a jig,
The sun's a clown, doing a gig.
Birds dive in with a splash of cheer,
While I sip coffee, the humor's near.

Flip-flops flapping, I dance on the sand,
Chasing shadows that prance, oh so grand.
Crabs doing the hustle, a sight to behold,
Even the seashells seem to laugh and be bold.

Glimmering Palms in the Evening Light

Palms wink at me with leaves so spry,
A lizard attempts a stand-up, oh my!
The sun paints the world in wacky hues,
While I chase my hat that's off on a cruise.

Cocktails giggle in glasses so bright,
A pineapple wearing shades feels just right.
With each sip I take, the giggles abound,
The whole beach erupts in laughter profound.

A Symphony of Cobalt and Gold

The waves are a band, so wild and fun,
Playing tunes to the beat of the sun.
Seashells dance, little twinkling stars,
While I humor a crab with my goofy guitars.

Laughter ripples across the whole shore,
A parrot croons, begging for encore.
Fish leap like comedians, splashing around,
Golden glimmers of joy in this merry sound.

Shores Adorned in Radiant Bliss

The beach is a stage, where giggles thrive,
Each wave is a joke, keeping us alive.
Sandy toes tap to the rhythm of fun,
Under the sun where the humor's never done.

Towels become capes, we're superheroes now,
On a quest for the best, and we don't know how.
Seagulls crack jokes as they steal my fries,
In this world filled with laughter, it's no surprise.

Gleaming Tides of the Heart

The waves dance high with glee,
As seagulls squawk a tune,
A crab wanders by, quite proud,
With a jaunty little swoon.

Flip-flops fly from sandy toes,
While laughter fills the air,
A beach ball bounces, then it goes,
Where's the cookie? Over there!

Whispering Sands Untold

The sun wears shades, it can't be beat,
As children build a fort,
But watch out, a wave might play,
And sweep away your court!

In the distance, a cat is caught,
Chasing its own tail,
It stops to think, then gets distraught,
And lands right on a snail!

Majesty in Mist and Sun

Here comes a boat with sails so bright,
It almost seems to sing,
But wait—a bird with snacks in sight,
Has turned it to a fling!

The drinks are high, the laughter loud,
As we chase the sunset glow,
Make sure you wear your silly crown,
Or the coolness won't bestow!

A Symphony of Light and Motion

A fish leaps high, a splash so grand,
It tickles all our fancies,
While dolphins join the merry band,
In synchronized romances.

The hourglass tips, the sand will flow,
As we dance under the sun,
Who knew that fun could make us glow,
Like jellybeans on the run!

Mosaic of Sea and Sun

In the ocean's dance, fish wear hats,
A clownfish grins, while seaweed chats.
Waves tickle shores with a giggle or two,
As seagulls perform their skyward revue.

Bikinis and board shorts, all mismatched,
The sand's a hot seat for toes that are scratched.
Flip-flops flip, causing quite a fuss,
As sunburned tourists catch ice cream bus.

Golden Threads Through Azure Pastures

On hammocks, we swing, sipping sweet tea,
Bugs join the party, oh so carefree.
Lizards wear sunglasses, strut to the beat,
While flamingos dance with uncoordinated feet.

A pineapple hat becomes all the rage,
As coconuts burst from their leafy cage.
Sandy hairdos defy every rule,
The sun has summoned each silly fool.

Encounters on the Edge of Dusk

At twilight's whisper, crabs throw a rave,
As the sun winks out from its oceanic grave.
The stars twinkle down with a playful glare,
While dolphins choose dance partners with flair.

Laughter erupts from a firefly swarm,
Roasting marshmallows takes on a new form.
As the moon takes stage in the darkening sky,
A firegrass band plays sweet lullaby.

Celestial Shores of a Sunset Promise

Shells hold secrets of gossiping tides,
As starfish claim thrones on the surf's wild slides.
Umbrellas spin tales of sunscreen fights,
While sunset paints worlds with neon lights.

Children chase waves like they're chasing dreams,
Turning sandcastles to watery schemes.
A parrot squawks jokes, more silly than clever,
As sunset promises fun forever.

Gleaming Shores of Bliss

Sandy toes and laughter loud,
Seagulls strutting, feeling proud.
A crab in shades, it did a dance,
While sunbathers glared, lost in trance.

Ice cream drips on shining skin,
Where's my towel? Did it swim?
Flip-flops flying, quite the show,
But who knew toes could be so low?

Waves that giggle, tickle, tease,
Splashing drinks meant for the breeze.
Sunshine shorts, and hats so grand,
A sunburned nose, can you understand?

Eat your lunch – it's mobile, too!
Sandwich chaos in a stew.
The perfect spot for sandy chips,
As gulls swarm in for tasty nips.

Jewel-Toned Refuge

A hammock sways, but I can't nap,
As bugs perform their buzzing rap.
Coconuts fall with monstrous thuds,
Should I dodge or just play buds?

Socks and sandals, quite the sight,
What's that smell? A fish in flight?
My shades are bright, my mood is light,
But my beach ball took an epic flight.

Palm trees whisper, gossip low,
"Who's that guy with the sunburn glow?"
Shells abound but where's the loot?
I traded flip-flops for a fruit!

Fishy faces, topping the fun,
Underwater races, everyone run!
Laugh until the sun goes down,
For silly fun is summer's crown.

Sunlight on Sapphire Seas

A splash of joy, a splash of glee,
Fish in shades, they swim with me.
Surfboards wobble like jelly beans,
While dolphins tease in sunny scenes.

Sunscreen fails, my nose is bright,
I guess a lobster's quite the sight.
Drinks adorned with umbrellas small,
Can this really happen? Oh, y'all!

With sandcastles high and dreams to share,
Seagulls plotting from the air.
"Is that my sandwich? What a theft!"
While kids just giggle, holding breath.

Catch the waves, or catch a breeze,
Water fights that bring us ease.
Laughing till we turn all red,
In this vibrant dream, we tread.

The Dance of Light and Water

Sunshine wiggles on the shore,
With every wave, I laugh and roar.
Splashing feet, a ticklish game,
But who put a clam in the fame?

Underwater selfies, woes abound,
As funny faces twist around.
A mermaid here with shells to boast,
But really, I just want some toast!

Belly flops and cannonballs,
As laughter echoes down the halls.
With every splash, friends lost in fun,
We're all just kids under the sun.

Crab that dances with a flair,
Who tied that string in my hair?
Twinkling waves and golden rays,
Life's a party, hip-hip-hoorays!

Shifting Shadows of Delicate Luminescence

In the land where colors play,
Feet dance on the sandy ballet.
Flamingos might just wear a bow,
While jellyfish gracefully flow.

Banana peels on coral reefs,
Giggling fish share silly chief.
Seashells whisper jokes so light,
As wise crabs sing into the night.

Palm trees sway with feathered hats,
Bicycles race with squawking bats.
A sunbeam slides on coconut,
Swapping secrets with a nut.

Bubbles bounce in merriment,
As seagulls join in the content.
With laughter ringing like a bell,
This vibrant dream still casts a spell.

Celestial Colors in Motion

The sky's a canvas, bright and wild,
Where painted clouds dance like a child.
Parrots juggle with their wings,
As jesters in the sun's sweet rings.

A starfish strums a ukulele,
While sea cucumbers act so gaily.
Coconuts hold parties on the shore,
With limbo sticks and open doors.

Laughter bounces off the waves,
As the tide rolls in, it misbehaves.
Bright fish wear hats that bob and weave,
While crabs crack jokes no one believes.

With colors splashed from sky to sea,
The world's a circus, wild and free.
Under a sun with a cheeky grin,
Life here's a jest where joy begins.

The Heavens Between Water and Sand

Where the waves meet golden hues,
Seashells chatter with the news.
Octopuses paint with brilliant flair,
As seabirds dive through salty air.

A crab in sunglasses strolls the beach,
Sipping lemonade, oh what a reach!
With twinkling eyes, the starfish yells,
"Count the sandcastles, can't you tell?"

The sun flips pancakes, shiny bright,
While a dolphin takes a graceful flight.
Gulls compete with fish for a laugh,
In this quirky, sunny photograph.

As shadows dance in hues so bold,
The sea shares secrets, never told.
Beneath the sparkles and sun-kissed glow,
Life's a party, don't you know?

An Oasis of Bright Perspectives

In the midst of colors so absurd,
Cacti try their best to be heard.
Lizards compete for the tallest hat,
While a parrot mimics a chitchat.

Rainbows stretch across the sky,
As laughter soars, you know why.
With pineapple pizza, a tasty treat,
Even the ants get up on their feet.

Under a sun that loves to tease,
Balloons float around like bees.
The sand tickles toes in silly games,
While lizards perform their acrobatic claims.

There's joy in the breeze, a maraca sound,
As shimmering sunsets come around.
In this lively land of vivid hue,
Every moment's a giggle, just for you.

Secrets in the Shimmering Silence

In the quiet, fish are laughing,
Turtles toss their shells with glee.
A crab winks with a snappy hard hand,
While the seaweed dances, full of spree.

Stars twinkle down like candy wrappers,
As dolphins play tag with a wink.
The waves tickle toes of beachgoers,
In a splash that makes you rethink.

Seagulls squawk in a silly chorus,
They strut and hop, such clumsy grace.
Every grain of sand is laughing,
Join the party, it's a wild place!

The sun sets low, a golden grin,
Nighttime tickles with a breeze.
The magic here is ever-spinning,
With secrets hidden in the seas.

Warm Breezes and Aqua Dreams

Warm winds tease the silly palm trees,
As coconuts tumble with a thud.
The sun is a jester in a bright hat,
While waves burble like a cheeky bud.

Flip-flops chatter on the hot sand,
As friends play tag with a beach ball.
Sandcastles rise with royal flair,
Until a little wave makes them fall!

Ice creams melt on sticky fingers,
While laughter rolls like ocean swells.
A hermit crab joins in the fun,
Clutching his shell with giggly shells.

Stars are the confetti of night,
As fireflies flicker in delight.
With every dance, the world feels lighter,
Tomorrow holds more fun, just right!

An Ode to Light and Shade

Sunbeams bounce off a dancing dolphin,
While shadows stretch like sleepy cats.
The palm trees sway in a playful jig,
And the sun whispers silly chats.

A beach ball rolls, a runaway,
Chasing laughter all through the tide.
With flip-flops flying in the frenzy,
It's a wild ride, let's enjoy the slide!

Shells scatter secrets on the shore,
And seagulls laugh like feathered fiends.
A hammock swings, so cozy and warm,
While the sun plots giggles and dreams.

The beach is a stage; let's all perform,
Under the sky of candy-colored skies.
As sunset paints with swirls of joy,
Every moment is a happy surprise!

Rippling Reflections in Lavish Colors

Mirrors of water gleam with laughter,
While fish wear hats and dance around.
A jellyfish sways in a goofy way,
As starfish giggle without a sound.

Mangoes tumble off the lunch tray,
As beach balls bounce in playful arcs.
With every splash, a funny face,
And bright flip-flops mark the parks.

The sunset drips with colors so bold,
Like a painter gone grinning mad.
It splashes joy upon each wave,
Making the whole world feel glad.

Under stars that twinkle with cheer,
The night hums a playful tune.
Every creature joins in the fun,
Together we sway beneath the moon.

Echoes of the Cerulean Breeze

Seagulls squawk like they own the place,
While crabs run a race, all out of pace.
A sandcastle king, with a jellyfish crown,
Waves come to steal him, oh, what a frown!

Flip-flops flapping, a dance on the shore,
A beach ball bounces, then rolls out the door.
Sun hats are flying, oh what a scene,
As sunscreen lovers turn into a sheen!

Palm trees sway, saying, 'Aloha, friend!'
While kids giggle loud, their giggles won't end.
An octopus juggles seashells in style,
Who knew beach days could bring such a smile?

Hermit crabs holding a shell fashion show,
With seaweed belts that steal the whole show.
The breeze whispers jokes only fish understand,
With laughter and splashes that sparkle the sand!

Glistening Sands at Twilight

As dusk unfolds, the crickets share jokes,
Cocktails are shaking, with fruity yolks.
A sunset parade, all orange and pink,
As sunburned tourists stare, then blink!

Chairs are stacked high in a wobbly way,
As hats fly off, come join the display!
Tropical drinks, with umbrellas galore,
One sip too many, they're out on the floor!

Fireflies twinkle, a disco of light,
While sandcastles giggle, feeling quite right.
A beach ball's gone rogue, rolling with glee,
Causing chaos where all can see!

Mounds of laughter, oh, what a sight,
As surfers and mermaids dance in delight.
The moon plays tricks, reflecting the waves,
In a playful world where silliness saves!

Sun-kissed Currents of Joy

With surfboards waiting, like dogs for a treat,
The ocean calls out, 'Come dance on my feet!'
Flippers flapping like silly old clowns,
As whales sing ballads, they wear giddy frowns!

Coconuts rolling in a rib-tickling chase,
While flip-flops flop, setting a silly pace.
Seashells conspire to steal all the fame,
The water's a playground, a hilarious game!

Twinkling starfish, hosting a rave,
In the splash zone, all laughter is brave.
Fishermen's tales grow taller each night,
As mermaids chuckle at their fishy plight!

Seagulls audition for a sitcom role,
While beachcombers hunt for a buried bowl.
A lobster wearing glasses strolls with a wink,
In a world of giggles, let's raise a drink!

The Hues of Paradise Found

Bright parrots gossip, spreading the news,
Of a crab who dances in flamboyant shoes.
Mangoes juggle on a picnic spread,
As tourists take naps, dreaming of bread!

The sun bakes all, but what a delight,
As laughter erupts with each sparkly bite.
Sunscreen tags team up to steal the show,
While sand squirrels argue about where to go!

In a hammock, two turtles share a grand tale,
Of a snail who once rode a wild wave trail.
Bananas take turns on a swing made of leaves,
As laughter erupts, oh, how the heart believes!

Jumping porpoises, the ocean's delight,
Dance with the waves, oh, what a sight!
In the colors of laughter, we find surprise,
In a paradise painted with giggling skies!

Nature's Amber Symphony

A parrot squawks, it's lost its sock,
The monkey laughs, what a funny shock.
Palm trees sway, doing the twist,
While crabs do their dance, can't be missed.

Sunshine blinks, is it just a game?
Seagulls gossip, spreading some fame.
Coconuts fall with a thump and a roll,
As turtles juggle, it takes quite a toll!

Colorful fish wear hats made of sea,
They swim 'round in style, so fancy and free.
A hermit's mad dash to claim his new shell,
While dolphins ring bells, all's perfect and swell.

A breeze whispers jokes that the flowers can share,
The sun beams down with a mischievous glare.
Nature's laughter rings from tree to bay,
Join in the fun, let's all shout hooray!

Dreams in Cerulean

A fish in a vest, what a curious sight,
Swims past a turtle, who's lost in delight.
Clouds doing karaoke, what a raucous show,
The seaweed sways high, putting on a glow.

Crabs in a band, making music so loud,
Dance on the shore, captivating the crowd.
A beach ball ascends, it's taking a flight,
Laughter erupts, what a joyous delight!

Seashells gossip, oh, what do they say?
A seagull forgot how to fly straight today.
The sun plays peekaboo, hiding just right,
While everyone giggles at the silly sight.

As day turns to night, the fun won't cease,
With fireflies winking, they light up the peace.
In dreams we all frolic, as stars twinkle near,
Nature invites us, come celebrate here!

A Glimmer Beneath the Canopy

Beneath the green arch, a rabbit pulls tricks,
Wearing a bow tie, he shows off his kicks.
Squirrels gossip over acorn pie,
As fireflies dance, putting on a fly.

Chameleons, stylish, change color and groove,
As frogs leap about, they've got all the moves.
A skunk in a hat adds to the flair,
While butterflies giggle, floating in air.

The sun peeks through leaves with a cheeky grin,
A snake cracks a joke, all the critters join in.
What's the best dance? The limbo, they say,
So much to enjoy, come join in the play!

With laughter and cheers, the canopy beams,
A magical world, more fun than it seems.
Nature's own circus is lively and bright,
Under the green arch, it's pure sheer delight!

The Polished Jewel of Dusk

As the day bows out, stars begin to blink,
An owl hoots loudly, it winks and it drinks.
Fireflies flash like they're on a quest,
As crickets chirp jokes, they're quite the best!

A raccoon in boots struts down the path,
With snacks in his hands, oh, what a laugh!
The moon plays a tune that's jazzy and cool,
While night critters gather, they're breaking the rules.

Laughter erupts as a fox tells a tale,
Of mischief and fun, where no one can fail.
The breeze gives a shiver, a tickle delight,
As nature's own party goes on through the night.

With colors so rich and humor in flow,
The polished jewel shines, giving a glow.
Join in the wonder, let's dance and explore,
In this enchanted dusk, you'll find so much more!

Golden Horizons in Aqua Skies

A parrot sings in shades of cheer,
He steals my drink and shouts, "I'm here!"
The sun slips down, a golden fry,
While crabs do the limbo, oh my, oh my!

With flip-flops flapping, laughter rings,
A fish with sunglasses, oh the bling!
Each wave whispers a joke so sly,
As dolphins dance, and seagulls fly!

A coconut falls, don't be in shock,
It lands right here, just near my sock.
With every splash, the fun just grows,
Who knew the beach had such shows?

So raise a toast to sandy toes,
To fruity drinks and silly prose.
As laughter drips like melting ice,
We'll take our fun, no need for spice!

Radiant Reflections on Still Waters

In a kayak made of marshmallow fluff,
I paddled hard; this is quite tough!
With glittering fish that wink with glee,
They swim around like they know me!

The sun beams down with a playful grin,
While frogs on lily pads dance and spin.
A turtle strolls, oh what a sight,
Wearing a bow tie, he's dressed just right!

Bubbles rise as the wind does tease,
I caught a breeze, but where's my cheese?
As butterflies giggle and whirl in flight,
This whimsical world feels just so right!

With ripples forming a charming show,
Who needs a movie? We've got the flow!
So join the fun, come share a laugh,
On this lake parade, we're all a gaffe!

Sun-Kissed Horizons

Sunshine bounces on the beach so bright,
With a piña colada, I feel all right.
A crab in my sandal looks quite absurd,
He twirls around like he's got the word!

With waves that giggle and tickle toes,
A seagull swoops and knows how it goes.
It snatches my fries without a care,
That thieving bird, I'll chase him bare!

Sandy castles rise like fluffy cakes,
While a kid quickly learns that water shakes.
He dives right in with a splash so grand,
Leaving his towel to wash up on land!

So let's embrace the sun's bright smile,
And dance on the shore for a little while.
With each wave crashing, our laughter flows,
In this sunny realm where pure joy grows!

Azure Serenity Beneath the Palms

Underneath the palms, I find my seat,
With a coconut drink and a cheeky repeat.
The breeze brings whispers of a silly tune,
While lizards boogie on a sun-warmed dune.

A sun hat flies, it takes to the sky,
Chased by a crab who thinks he can fly.
The shadows dance while clouds prance by,
Who knew a beach day could make you cry?

With hammock swaying like a big soft hug,
I swing to laughter, feeling quite snug.
A fish pops up, with a wink and smile,
It splashes my drink; it's all worth the trial!

So, join the fun, bring your best cheer,
This paradise whispers, "Come have a beer!"
With smiles and giggles as our only goal,
Let's bask in the warmth and let laughter roll!

Shoreline Serenade

Waves crash and the seagulls squawk,
Sandcastles melt in a gentle floc,
Crabs dance sideways in a quirky trot,
While sunscreen slips, we all forgot!

Flip-flops slapping, they're quite a cheer,
Sandy toes are a sign of a good year,
Chasing ice cream with sticky glee,
Oh, the joys of being free!

Beach balls bounce, much to their dismay,
They roll away, but we laugh and play,
A splash of water, a yelp from me,
Life's a giggle, can't you see?

Under the sun, with laughter we glow,
Sipping on coconut, moving slow,
Oh, what a circus, all in a row,
On this bright shore, we steal the show!

The Warmth of Luminous Laughter

Sunshine beams on my sunburned nose,
Tickling my thoughts, it merrily goes,
Ice cream drips down, a colorful trail,
Laughter erupts, it cannot fail!

Bikini blunders and flip-flop flops,
Moments like these are the cream of the crop,
Sunscreen battles lead to laughter galore,
In this radiant madness, we simply adore!

Grass skirts twirl in a wobbly dance,
Hilarity strikes at a chance romance,
Bumping into shadows, we giggle away,
Finding the joy in each silly play!

Glow sticks glow as the night takes a leap,
With raucous laughter, we don't miss a beat,
Roasted marshmallows turn into a mess,
Yet we share stories and laugh, no stress!

In the Embrace of Dappled Sunlight

Lazy hammocks sway in the breeze,
Morning coffee dribbles with ease,
Squirrels jump and chase with delight,
As sunlight nudges the day into bright!

Picnic blankets, all scattered and tossed,
Sandwiches vanish, oh, what a cost!
Limes hit the floor, we hear a loud splat,
Watch your step, or it's a slippery chat!

Kites are flying, oh what a sight,
But one tangled tail causes a fight,
Giggles arise as we wrestle with strings,
In this dappled bliss, the laughter just sings!

Lemonade smiles, the drinks overflow,
Every sip brings laughter's sweet glow,
In the shade's embrace, we smile and play,
Sharing these moments on a sunlit day!

Hues of Harmony

Rainbow colors splash on a canvas bright,
Dancing paintbrushes, oh what a sight,
Jelly beans scatter as ideas take flight,
Creating a world where laughter ignites!

Bowls of fruit, a colorful mess,
With every nibble, it turns to finesse,
But watch out for splatters, they land with a thud,
And soon we're all painted—a rainbow of fun!

Tie-dye shirts blend in the sun's warm hue,
Mismatched patterns, oh who knew?
Stumbling and laughing, we trip on our joy,
Creating memories no one can destroy!

As evening falls, our colors still swirl,
With stories and giggles, let laughter unfurl,
In this vibrant mix, where harmony shines,
A tapestry woven with friendship that binds!

Melodies of Sunlit Waters

In the splash of waves, fish wear bright hats,
Splashing at seagulls who steal their spats.
Crabs dance like crazy, all sideways and fast,
While dolphins giggle, their laughter will last.

Beneath the warm glow, the sun's up to tricks,
As seaweed plays tag with some glittery sticks.
A clam holding court shows off his fine pearls,
As nearby, a turtle winks at the swirls.

There's a parrot who croons in a tree overhead,
Telling tales of adventures, or so it is said.
With salsa and limbo, the coconuts sway,
As pineapples rock out to a conga ballet.

In this silly kingdom where laughter ensues,
The ocean's a stage, and everyone hues.
With echoes of joy in the splash of the blue,
We dance in the sunshine, just me and my crew.

Where Sea Meets Ember

As sunset spills gold on the wavy front,
A crab wears sunglasses—oh, what a stunt!
Flip-flops are lost in the pebbles and sand,
While the jellyfish jiggles, oh isn't it grand?

With popcorn clouds drifting in peachy delight,
The gulls hold a party in the fading light.
One gull takes a dive—he thinks he's a fish,
But flops with a splash, oh, a memorable wish!

The breeze starts to snicker, the waves call for cheer,
As the sunset turns purple, the night holds no fear.
Laughter mingles sweetly with the firefly glow,
While they sway to the rhythm of a laid-back show.

So raise a soft drink, let's toast to the night,
With characters silly and nature in sight.
As stars join the fun in a sparkling hue,
We laugh till it's morning, with skies oh so blue.

The Gilded Horizon Awaits

Palm trees are gossiping, what will they wear?
A coconut struts with a new golden flair.
Fluffy clouds scatter like candy on high,
While crabs throw confetti, oh my, oh my!

The sun is a jester, it plays peek-a-boo,
As laughter erupts from a bright-colored crew.
A pelican juggles with shells on his beak,
While fish make a splash for a mask and a streak.

The horizon giggles as day turns to night,
With twinkling surprises that feel just so right.
A bonfire's a beacon of warmth and of cheer,
As dreams take their flight in the warmth of the sphere.

So let's dance with the shadows and sing with the breeze,
To the sound of the waves whispering through trees.
With hearts full of mirth, let's celebrate now,
For the horizon awaits, we'll join in the wow!

Echoes of a Vibrant Dawn

As sunbeams tickle the ocean awake,
The fish throw a party, for laughter's at stake.
A parrot is blabbering jokes to the tide,
While waves toss confetti, all sparkly and wide.

The sandcastles giggle, they know what's at play,
With seashells as guests making merry all day.
Lobsters are dancing in bright polka dots,
While sea turtles swirl in their best funky pots.

The sun winks slyly, as it plays with the day,
While starfish hold hands, a quirky ballet.
With laughter erupting like bubbles from deep,
They prank all the vacationers lost in the sweep.

So let's greet the morn with a skip and a spin,
Where the sea joins the chorus and laughter begins.
In this wacky utopia of happiness bright,
We'll dance on the shoreline till the fall of the night.

Reflections of a Sun-Seeker

I chased the rays with sunscreen on,
A slip, a slide, then off I'm gone.
In flip-flops dancing through the sand,
I can't believe I lost my brand!

A coconut gave me quite a fright,
As I laughed, took a sip, felt alright.
But soon it rolled and hit my foot,
I'm off the cliff… but wait, I'm soot!

The sunshine's bright, I'm feeling bold,
But then my ice cream starts to fold.
It drips and drops, my shirt's a mess,
At least I wear my colors 'best'!

As golden beams warm up the day,
I giggle loud, then run away.
For every splash and every fall,
I'll revel in the sun and all!

The Palette of Paradise

In a world where colors collide,
I wore a hat that's way too wide.
With shades of yellow, pink, and green,
My fashion sense? Well, it's unseen!

The parrots laugh as I parade,
Creating shadows in the glade.
My mismatched socks and polka dots,
Are a sight to see, and hit the spots!

A painter's brush begins to swirl,
I trip on waves, oh what a whirl!
With colors splashing on my face,
Who knew the beach would be a race?

Each sunset hums a funny tune,
While sandcastles dream of the moon.
I laugh, I dance, I stand in glee,
In palettes bold as life's to be!

Warmth of the Setting Sun

The sun dips low, the sky's ablaze,
I chase the hues through silly ways.
With spaghetti strands of beachy hair,
I trip on towels, it's quite a scare!

Ice cream melts, and laughter rings,
As crabs invite us to their flings.
I slide on shells, a graceful flop,
Is it the sun, or just a drop?

Banana boats that glide with glee,
But I steer left, they flee from me!
My friends are laughing, what a sight,
I dance beneath the fading light.

A golden glow wraps me right up,
While bubbles float, I take a cup.
With warmth on cheeks, we'll sing and sway,
Till stars pop out to join our play!

Tranquility in a Sea of Color

In a cove where colors blend and twist,
I wore a crown made of jellyfish.
With seaweed braids and a silly grin,
I thought that ocean waves could win!

The pelicans join my goofy dance,
They flap about in a clumsy trance.
I swirl and twirl with fins at play,
While jellybeans bounce my cares away!

With sunsets painting skies so bright,
I stumbled 'round, my shoes feel light.
The ocean giggles as I slip,
Down to the waves, I make a dip!

But joy is found where laughter flows,
In a sea of color, watch it grow.
With every splash, I find my roll,
In fits of fun, I lose control!

Dance of the Sapphire Sirens

In the waves, they sway and prance,
With mismatched socks, they do their dance,
A flip-flop here, a coconut there,
Laughing loudly without a care.

With pearly shells they make a sound,
A giggle here, a gurgle found,
They lure the fish with silly songs,
And turn the seaweed into throngs.

Their voices echo, bright and clear,
As crabs join in, with lots of cheer,
In fins and flippers, what a sight,
Under the sun, all day and night.

As dolphins leap, they spin and twirl,
Each joyful wave, they whirl and swirl,
Those mischief-makers of the sea,
Bring smiles and laughter, wild and free.

Whispers Beneath the Golden Canopy

Beneath the leaves, two parrots chat,
One wears glasses, the other a hat,
They trade funny tales of fruit and fun,
And compete on how fast they can run.

A monkey swings from branch to branch,
In fuzzy socks, he starts to prance,
He slips and flips, a comical show,
As laughter weaves through the trees below.

The sunbeams dance on the forest floor,
Where critters gather, eager for more,
They hold a party, snacks galore,
With giggles and nibbles, who could ask for more?

In this golden glow, all creatures play,
Each moment is bright, and none want to stray,
With kooky antics and songs in the air,
The world's a circus, laughter to share.

Azure Dreams and Radiant Skies

On a cloud of candy, jellybeans ride,
With sprinkles of laughter, they glide and slide,
A rainbow unicorn leads the brigade,
While gumball trees shade their parade.

They toss confetti made from fluff,
And dodge the pie that's gooey and tough,
As they roll in giggles, the sun's shining high,
Painting the world as they bounce from the sky.

With blueberry waves and a lollipop breeze,
They make wishes with the utmost ease,
A serenade sung by the jellyfish band,
Bringing joy and fun to the colorful land.

In these dreams painted bright, they leap and race,
Chasing the clouds at a jocular pace,
With every chuckle, the skies grow wide,
As laughter echoes, like a joyful tide.

Harmony of Light and Ocean

In the tide pools, crabs throw a bash,
With seaweed hats, they dance and splash,
A fish with sunglasses gives a wink,
As the starfish plots to pour them a drink.

The waves giggle as they tickle the shore,
While shells chime in with a clattering score,
They twirl with laughter, the sea's own crew,
As a jellyfish juggles, giving a view.

With a twinkling glow, the sun starts to set,
Creating shadows, making a bet,
Who'll catch the silliest crab in a net?
With fun in their hearts, they'll never fret.

In harmony, the ocean sings,
With flippers and fins, the joy it brings,
Together they dance, in glitter and glee,
A fabulous party, come join the spree!

Turquoise Waves and Sunlit Dreams

In a land where coconuts sing,
The sun wears a crown, oh what a thing!
Surfboards dance like clumsy fish,
Waves giggle, granting each wild wish.

Seagulls squawk, wearing shades of cool,
Chasing crabs as they break the rule.
Sandcastles bow to a water fate,
While flip-flops make their great escape.

Beach chairs lounge, sipping mocktail bliss,
As sandmen ponder their sculptor's kiss.
The sun winks like it knows some tricks,
And sunscreen battles against the licks.

With toes in the ocean, laughter flows,
Beachcombers giggle, striking goofy poses.
A hammock sways, the breeze a tease,
In paradise, we swing with ease.

Luminous Hues of Serendipity

Balloons bounce under a marigold sun,
Whimsical kites dance—oh, what fun!
Fish wear costumes, bright and bold,
Trying to fish for compliments told.

Tropical birds, fashionably loud,
Mimic accents of a giggling crowd.
While sunburnt tourists search for shade,
A coconut falls—what a parade!

Laughter bubbles in every wave,
Swimmers float like jellybeans brave.
With floats shaped like flamingos, so chic,
Waves tumble over, it's playful and meek.

At sunset, we feast on piña coladas,
Juggling pineapples, oh what bravadas!
As stars twinkle, a gentle nudge,
Life's a comedy, we can't help but judge.

Caribbean Whisperings

The goofy parrot tells silly tales,
Of treasure maps lost in the gales.
Mangoes play tag with the breeze,
While beachgoers aim for a breeze with ease.

Funky fish wear hats made of seaweed,
Competing in style, they take the lead.
Sand dollars giggle as they roll,
Playing hide and seek, that's their goal.

With ice cream dribbles on beach shorts bright,
Kids chase the waves, a comical sight.
As sunsets splash colors like confetti,
A dance party blooms, so light and petty.

The steel drums play a whimsical tune,
While crabs shake it under the moon.
In this laughter-laden shore so wild,
Every moment feels like a wished-for child.

Celestial Sands at Dusk

Under the twilight, where shadows prance,
The sand winks back, joining the dance.
Starfish giggle, twinkling their best,
While beach balls roll out for a jest.

Glow-in-the-dark shells compete for attention,
Shimmering soft, they spark sweet invention.
Frolicking turtles try to break speed,
Fumbling around, it's a joyful creed.

As bonfires crackle, shadows reply,
The marshmallow wars escalate high.
With laughter and jokes, the night unfolds,
While funny stories of fish are retold.

In this sandy embrace, with friends all new,
Each wave whispers secrets—and maybe a boo!
Life's a zany drama under the stars,
In a place where reality meets caviar.

Echoes of Paradise

In the land where coconuts fall,
The parrots squawk and have a ball.
Sunblock sloshed on, looking quite bright,
I resemble a lobster, not quite a sight.

Flip-flops flapping, the dance is a thrill,
I trip on a wave, now I'm part of the still.
Seagulls are laughing, I join in the fun,
Who knew that beach life could really weigh a ton?

The piña coladas are calling my name,
But I spill them all, and it's me that is to blame.
A wave crashes in; I scream in surprise,
Sandy hair, goofy grin, oh what a disguise!

The hammock swings low, I take a quick nap,
My dreams are of dolphins, then I fall with a flap.
Waking to laughter, my friends in a fit,
They snap a quick photo, I'm now a big hit!

Ocean's Warm Embrace

The ocean waves tickle my toes,
I chase down a crab who obviously knows.
With flip-flops in hand, I jump with a yell,
Falling face-first, my pride is a shell.

The sun is a blanket, so warm on my skin,
I forgot the sunscreen—oops! Where to begin?
The laughter of children, they flop all around,
I join in the chaos, it's pure joy unbound.

The beach umbrella, I thought it was grand,
Turns inside out, it's now a sailboat in sand.
With a swimsuit so loud, a spectacle seen,
I'm saving the world in my bright shades of green.

A sandwich I packed just for the day,
But the gull saw my treasure and flew it away.
I sit on the shore, a victim of fate,
With salt on my fries and laughter innate.

Rift of Oceanic Radiance

With a cooler of snacks, I venture outside,
The beach is my kingdom, my fortress, my pride.
Watching the surfboards dance on the waves,
I'm glued to my towel, where comfort enslaves.

A crab made a dash, I let out a scream,
Turns out it's just Tom in his new swimming theme.
The shades I sport could blind you with glee,
Reflecting my laughter, whoever sees me.

The sun has a schedule, it starts to descend,
I wonder how long till my day starts to end.
But then comes the sunset, a colorful blur,
Like cotton candy painted in pinks and a spur.

I build up a castle, it topples with grace,
The tide's not my friend, it's quite the disgrace.
But here with my pals, I'm a king on my throne,
In this rift of delight, I've truly outgrown!

When the Sea Meets the Sun

In the morning light, the horizon awakes,
I'm half in my dream while the rooster shakes.
Paddle boards drift like a scene from a dream,
While I'm battling waves—what's the score? Just a meme.

Sandy snacks scattered, my lunch flies away,
Chasing after seagulls—oh, what a day!
The treasure I found was buried in the sand,
A flip-flop, a shell, and a rubber band.

I attempted to surf, but I fell on my face,
The ocean just giggles as I drown in disgrace.
A beach ball rolls past; I give it a kick,
Now I'm the star of this comedy flick!

But as the sun sets, it's all smiles and cheer,
With friends all around, so much joy in the years.
I laugh with the waves and dance with the breeze,
Life's a hilarious ride; I'm ready to seize!

Whispers of Azure Waves

The ocean calls with silly glee,
Fishes giggle, oh so free!
Seagulls dance on sun-kissed foam,
While crabs play tag, far from home.

Waves waltz in a playful race,
Sunbathers laugh as they embrace!
A dolphin pops up, grinning wide,
Playing peek-a-boo with the tide.

Sandcastles tumble in a flop,
A toddler's laughter never stops!
Mermaids tease with glittered tails,
While jellyfish roll in comedic gales.

So grab a drink, let's share a cheer,
In this paradise, spread the cheer!
With every splash, each silly stunt,
Life's a beach, come join the hunt!

Sunlit Shores and Sapphire Skies

On warm sands, the sunbeams play,
Beach balls bounce in a bright ballet!
Shells wear hats that clams adore,
While surfers fall with a mighty roar.

Laughter echoes, a comical tune,
As crabs march under the lazy moon!
A toucan drops its snack in haste,
Creating a scene, oh what a waste!

Umbrellas tilt like hats askew,
Sunset paints the sky in a hue.
A sandman waves with a goofy grin,
As kites twist in the breeze, let the fun begin!

So raise your drinks and hold them high,
To funny moments beneath the sky!
With each silly slip, our spirits lift,
In laughter's embrace, we find our gift.

Golden Horizons at Dusk

As evening falls, the glow ignites,
The horizon bumbles, what a sight!
Frogs in tuxedos jump in style,
While fireflies dance, making us smile.

Sandy toes and quirky hats,
A parrot squawks while looking for rats!
Sunset nachos on plates of shells,
As laughter' sings and giggles swell.

The moon slips in with a silver grin,
Tickling waves, let the fun begin!
Sandpipers strut with a royal air,
While the breeze swirls around without a care.

So gather 'round, share a tale or two,
Let sandy shenanigans come to view!
With every chuckle, the night is young,
In the glow of laughter, we've just begun!

Serenade of the Aquatic Breezes

Waves whisper quirky serenades,
As fish in hats dance in parades!
Turtles spin in a confused swirl,
While starfish sport a fashionable twirl.

Breezes laugh, tickling the palm,
Dancers shake to the ocean's calm!
Shrimps break out in a conga line,
As crabs provide the punch, oh so fine!

Splashing about with a joyful shout,
Each splash brings laughter, there's no doubt!
Seashells collecting giggles and sighs,
As the sunset paints whimsical skies.

So come and join this joyous spree,
Where smiles float as wild and free!
Let's sing along with the breezy tunes,
In this aquatic laughter, beneath the moons!

Illuminated Shores of Nostalgia

Seagulls dance like silver spoons,
While crabs play tag beneath the dunes.
The waves whisper tales of old,
As sandcastle dreams start to fold.

A flip-flop lands in the sea,
Its owner shouts, "Come back to me!"
But the fish just giggle and swim away,
Ignoring the plea for another day.

The children chase the sunset's tail,
Each one hoping to find a whale.
But it's just a buoy bobbing about,
As laughter erupts in joyful shouts.

In the glow of a sunset's wink,
We toast with sodas, take a drink.
"To the sand! To the sea! To our silly crew!"
As the beach bums laugh and start anew.

The Canvas of the Day

Brushes dipped in sunshine bright,
Splashing colors left and right.
A coconut falls, a funny thud,
Plopping down with a satisfied 'smud.'

Palm trees wave like they're in a rave,
While sunscreen battles—'Who will save?'
The kids declare it a slippery fight,
As sand gets tossed with utmost delight.

A kite is tangled in a branch so high,
The owner is laughing—"I can fly!"
But gravity, my friend, has other plans,
As tangled up are the grown-up fans.

The sea, a canvas of giggles and peeps,
As the tide comes in, so the laughter leaps.
With beach balls bouncing, who can complain?
In our colorful world, all forget their pain.

The Sun's Kiss on the Ocean's Skin

The sun winks down, a playful tease,
While jellyfish float with graceful ease.
A splash, a giggle, someone gets wet,
A game of tag is firmly set.

A seagull flies off with a chip of fries,
Leaving behind disappointed eyes.
But laughter echoes as they all chase,
Sandy feet racing, it's a speedy race.

The waves roll in with a frothy grin,
Inviting the beachgoers to jump right in.
With cannonballs and silly squeals,
The day unfolds with all its appeals.

As sunset paints, we gather in line,
With ice cream cones that just can't align.
A sticky mess, but who really cares?
In this parade of joys, laughter flares.

Serenity in Spectrum

A hammock sways beneath the trees,
Where time forgets and worries freeze.
The breeze whispers jokes, a giggling breeze,
While ants parade by, as if to tease.

Chasing rainbows on the distant shore,
With flip-flops flying, the laughter in roar.
A dog dashes past with a towel in tow,
Its owner shouts, "Hey, that's not your show!"

Kites dip and dive, a colorful sight,
As the sun paints shadows of pure delight.
A picnic blanket turns to a magic mat,
Where sandwiches vanish, imagine that!

As the day fades to a whispering sigh,
With fireflies dancing against the sky.
We bask in the laughter, light as a feather,
Creating memories that last forever.

Reflections of Summer's Embrace

Bright umbrellas dance in the breeze,
Ice cream drips down with such ease.
Seagulls squawk, stealing a fry,
While sunbathers wail, 'Oh my, oh my!'

Laughter spills like soda pop,
Kids chase crabs along the top.
The sun, a big smile on display,
While waves giggle, 'Come out and play!'

Flip-flops flop, vacation vibes,
Sandy toes and jellyfish jibes.
As sunburns bloom like flowers in May,
We joke about our beach day spray!

Cocktails clink, with tiny umbrellas,
Mermaids laugh, they're quite the fellas.
In this sunlight, everything's bright,
Even the dolphins join in with delight.

The Tapestry of Dusk's Serenade

As the sun dips low, we all rush,
To see the glow, there's quite the hush.
Fireflies blink, a disco ball's delight,
While mosquitoes launch their evening flight.

In the twilight, stars begin their twirl,
We munch on snacks, giving fate a whirl.
S'mores make faces of melted glee,
As uncle Joe attempts to climb a tree.

Laughter echoes under the softening light,
Tales of yore included ghostly fright.
The campfire crackles, it lets out a cheer,
While marshmallows roast without a fear.

As the moon peeks down, we sing off-key,
Our voices blend, like waves in a spree.
In this dusky charm, the world feels right,
With funny blunders filling the night.

Serenade of Azure Shores

Waves giggle as they kiss the sand,
While crabs march in a tiny band.
Sunhat styles defy all fashion sense,
As sunscreen battles, a slippery offense.

Shells whisper secrets from tales untold,
While kiddos boast of treasures bold.
Mermaid sightings shift to a prank,
With a wave that leaves our spirits blank.

Kites swoop and swerve in the breeze,
As laughter bubbles, hearts find ease.
In flip-flops, we dance like silly fools,
Inventing new rules for beachside schools.

With ice-cold drinks in hand, we cheer,
Trading funny faces and shrimp-shaped gear.
When the sun sets, our joy's like a star,
Under moonbeams, we've traveled quite far.

Dawn's Radiant Embrace

Morning light peeks, a poky reprieve,
Coffee cups clink, 'Don't you believe?'
Jumping into day with such a splash,
Like a dolphin with a goofy dash.

Birds wake the world with their honks and tweets,
While we stumble out in our mismatched feats.
Pajamas on beach chairs, a stylish move,
As the sun rises, our spirits groove.

Socks with sandals? Absolutely okay!
The breakfast buffet is calling, 'Hooray!'
As we feast on fruits, and pancakes stack,
With syrup spills on our shirts, we won't look back.

As the day begins, adventures await,
With laughter and fun, we can't hesitate.
In the warmth of the sun, together we'll stay,
Chasing silly dreams till the end of the day.

Radiant Colors of Coastal Dreams

The ocean wears a silly hat,
A sunburned crab plays hide and chat.
Waves giggle as they splash the shore,
While seagulls race with snacks galore.

Flip-flops dancing, out of sync,
A daring dolphin starts to wink.
The sandcastles laugh with glee,
As the wind throws shells into the sea.

Beach umbrellas twist and shout,
Whispers of sun, let's turn about.
Sandy toes in a runway strut,
Skip and slide, who's in the rut?

The sunset paints a clownish grin,
A marshmallow sky where dreams begin.
While piña coladas frolic near,
Let's toast to laughter, bring the cheer!

Luminous Tides Beneath the Sun

Beneath the sun, a jellyfish prances,
Its bobbing dance leads to odd glances.
Surfboards slide like ticklish mice,
Each wave crashes, a splash of spice.

The young ones chase their dreams of gold,
While seagulls steal chips – oh, so bold!
Sunburns creep in on the unaware,
They'll rock those red lines with utmost flare.

Pool floats in shapes of cats and fries,
Synchronized swimming as laughter flies.
The skies giggle in a watercolor haze,
As sunshine leaves behind funny rays.

Lemonade spills, but who's to fret?
Each silly moment we shan't forget.
With wacky hats and splashes loud,
We'll dance with glee, so unbowed!

The Dance of Indigo Ripples

Ripples laugh as they ride the shore,
A fish flips out, yelling encore!
The starfish takes a break to nap,
While toddlers create a tidal trap.

Beach balls bounce with a bouncy cheer,
An octopus juggles without fear.
Sunscreens smeared like war paint bright,
A slip in the sand brings pure delight.

Sandy squirrels dig for surprise snacks,
As flip-flop marches leave funny tracks.
A tan line saga begins to sprout,
Where one arm's brown and the other – pout!

And when the day begins to fade,
Glow sticks light up the night parade.
With laughter echoing, we're all aglow,
In this sea of fun, we steal the show!

Warmth of Amber Reflections

The setting sun makes beaches blush,
While crabs compete in a funny rush.
With towels tangled, we lie around,
Creating stories from laughter's sound.

The water sparkles like disco lights,
As kids make friends with jelly delights.
Someone's hat goes flying high,
A boisterous "Catch it!" fills the sky.

A sunbather snores, lost in dreams,
While beach waves whisper wacky themes.
Ice cream drips, a delicious mess,
Leading to giggles, can't help but confess!

So hear the call of the sunset's swirl,
In this warm embrace, let laughter unfurl.
Wrap us in humor, let time stand still,
With each precious laugh, we feel the thrill!

The Allure of Sapphire Embraces

The ocean winks with a sparkle so bright,
And fish dance around, giving quite a sight.
A crab in a tux, with a dance of delight,
Claps claws to the rhythm, oh what a night!

With waves that giggle, and splashes that cheer,
A dolphin joins in, bringing smiles ear to ear.
Under the sun, all worries disappear,
Who knew such fun was the beach's career!

Seashells gossip of tales from the deep,
As sandy footprints lead to secrets they keep.
The sun, a big timer, takes leaps in a sweep,
While flip-flops bounce, in a dance not so steep!

In this paradise, where laughter takes flight,
The seagulls cackle, not caring for heights.
With drinks on ice, everything feels right,
And sunset's applause brings the end of the night!

Golden Memories Beneath the Palms

Beneath the tall trees where the shadows play,
A squirrel with style is munching away.
He wears tiny shades, oh what a display,
As beachgoers chuckle, not knowing his way!

The sun's on a break, taking selfies in gold,
While umbrellas whisper all the gossip untold.
A flip-flop goes missing, oh the drama unfolds,
As kids plot a treasure hunt, daring and bold!

The hammock sways gently, with laughter so light,
As someone gets tangled, what a funny sight!
The smoothies are blendered, with flavors so bright,
And pineapples giggle, it's quite a delight!

With golden memories stitched in the breeze,
Each smile is a treasure, no chance for unease.
As evening approaches, they all sing with ease,
Oh, life's a grand beach, where joy finds its keys!

Harmonics of Light and Water

Where the sun plays jazz and the waves hum a tune,
The sand's got some rhythm, more smooth than a boon.
A fish in a bowtie, he sways to the swoon,
And seaweed joins in, with a dance quite opportune!

Clouds puff like marshmallows, floats that drift by,
As a parrot recites all the latest sky-high.
While turtles debate on the shore's softest lie,
They giggle and snicker, oh my, oh my!

The laughter of children rings true like a bell,
As they chase after crabs, oh do tell, do tell!
With each tiny splash, it's a story to sell,
Of mermaids and pirates, in their own fairy spell!

As the sun dips low, with a wink and a kiss,
The night shares its secrets wrapped in bliss.
With stars joining in, it's a dance we can't miss,
Harmonics of life, what a sweet, funny twist!

Velvet Sky and Whispering Sea

The sky's a soft blanket, draped low and serene,
While the sea hums a tune, like a soothing machine.
A starfish conducts, with a wave and a sheen,
As bubbles take flight, in this whimsical scene!

Coconuts tumble, with tales to regale,
While gulls belt out ballads, in a light-hearted hail.
A crab with a monocle, setting up a sale,
As beachgoers chuckle, their laughter won't fail!

With sandcastles rising, a kingdom takes form,
As turtles train knights, oh what a norm!
Each wave sings a verse, in a playful swarm,
While the sun sets in glory, a perfect warm!

As night wraps the world, with a wink in its eye,
The glowworms come out, a brilliant supply.
With laughter like music, we dance and we sigh,
In this realm of delight, we're carefree and spry!

Aquamarine Reverie

In paradise where fish do dance,
A mermaid lost her only pants.
She giggles as she swims around,
In water's depths, her laughter's found.

With clamshells piled upon her head,
She claims a treasure made of bread.
The seahorses chuckle and tease,
While jellyfish wiggle with ease.

The starfish shout, 'Join in the fun!'
As crabs do cartwheels, one by one.
A conch shell sings a silly tune,
As dolphins dance beneath the moon.

And so in waves that twist and spin,
Our silly dreams and jokes begin.
In waters bright and full of cheer,
The joy of life is always near.

Harvest of Light

The sunbeams tease the coconut,
'You're more than just a place to shut!'
With palm trees swaying to the beat,
They dance and sway with wiggly feet.

The bananas giggle in their bunch,
Saying, 'Oh look! It's salad crunch!'
Pineapples wearing shades so bright,
Are plotting parties every night.

Come join the feast, let's have a ball,
With mangoes rolling down the hall.
The fruits all jive, the veggies cheer,
In laughter's glow, we find our gear.

So lift your forks and raise a toast,
For nature's fun we love the most.
In sunlight's warmth, we feel just right,
Come join us in this harvest light!

Kissed by the Waves

The ocean tickles toes and feet,
As sandy castles smell so sweet.
A crab's a sculptor, building tall,
While gulls scream, 'Don't you dare to fall!'

A beach ball flies high in the sky,
'Catch me!' it shouts, and won't say why.
With sunhats tilted to the side,
We dive into the waves with pride.

But seagulls swoop with silly squaw,
And steal the fries we held in awe.
Yet laughter drowns our petty woes,
As ocean breezes kiss our toes.

So here we splash and sing our songs,
In waves and laughter, we belong.
With tipsy tides that twist and play,
We're kissed by joy in every way.

Tides of Elysium

Where every shore brings laughter loud,
And seashells form a giggling crowd.
The tides do sway with funny grace,
As everyone joins in the chase.

The octopus plays checkers with crabs,
While seagulls flap and call us dabs.
The jellyfish wear tiny hats,
As starfish do their fancy chats.

A sand clown juggles shells with flair,
And everyone stops to stare.
His floppy shoes, a sight to see,
In this fun land where we roam free.

So here we frolic 'neath the sun,
Where silly games are never done.
In laughter's tides, we swim and play,
Creating joy in our own way.

The Glow of Coral Sunsets

As the sun dances, it's a silly sight,
Crabs put on hats, ready for the night.
The seagulls squawk, in a comical tune,
While fish wear sunglasses, under the moon.

A dolphin flips, with a wink and a grin,
Splashing the waves, let the laughter begin.
Starfish play poker, shells stack up high,
Funny little creatures, oh my oh my!

The horizon sparkles with giggles and cheer,
Whales tell jokes, everyone can hear.
Octopuses juggle, with arms in a spin,
In this wild circus, let the fun begin.

And as night falls, with a wink and a wave,
The sea becomes magic, oh how it behaves!
With a splash and a laugh, the day bids adieu,
In the glow of the sunset, life seems brand new.

Melodies of the Ocean's Heart

The ocean sings tunes, a humorous song,
With dolphins who dance and get it all wrong.
Waves tickle the shore, like a playful tease,
Seashells chuckle softly, riding the breeze.

A sea turtle winks, it's fashionably late,
While crabs on the beach are planning their fate.
The starfish tap dance, what a sight to behold,
Scattering laughter like glitter and gold.

Schools of fish giggle, in synchronized moves,
Flipping and flopping, they find their own grooves.
The jellyfish jiggle, in colorful flair,
Who knew the sea had such flair for a pair?

In the melody's rhythm, joy finds its place,
As waves crash with laughter, the ocean's embrace.
The beach is a stage, where all come to play,
In the symphony of life, it's a funny ballet.

Evening Skies in Brilliant Silk

The sky wears pajamas, a soft shade of blue,
As stars start to twinkle, they're in awe too.
Clouds look like marshmallows, fluffy and round,
A raccoon in a tutu prances on the ground.

The moon's a bright lantern, with a grin like a fool,
Casting shadows of critters, playing in the pool.
Fireflies are dancing, wearing fairy lights,
While frogs play in bands, performing all night.

The breeze is giggling, tickling the trees,
As owls are hooting, with a hint of tease.
In this vibrant tapestry, laughter unfurls,
With evening's soft charm, the world gently swirls.

So let's toast to the night in our whimsical way,
With cupcakes and stories, we'll play and we'll sway.
As silk blankets the skies, we'll dance 'til it's light,
In the heart of the fun, we'll claim our delight.

Flickers of Sunshine on Waves

The sun bobs and weaves, like a clumsy old chap,
With waves in a tizzy, they're caught in a flap.
Dolphins are laughing, with flips that amaze,
Splashing bright water, they're putting on plays.

Beachballs bounce high, without any care,
As sandcastles topple, in a hilarious flair.
Seagulls steal fries, with a cheeky little peep,
They waddle away, on their scavenger sweep.

Sun hats are flying, on the backs of the waves,
Where jellyfish dance like curious knaves.
In the sunlight's embrace, each moment's a jest,
In this sparkling world, we're all at our best.

So let's ride the tide, with laughter and glee,
In flickers of sunshine, be silly and free.
As waves tease the shore with their playful insist,
Join in the fun, it's too good to miss!

www.ingramcontent.com/pod-product-compliance
Lightning Source LLC
Chambersburg PA
CBHW072122070526
44585CB00016B/1527